WHO BUILT THE PYRAMIDS?

Jane Chisholm & Struan Reid

Illustrated by Sue Stitt

Designed by Vicki Groombridge & Diane Thistlethwaite

History consultant: Dr. Anne Millard
Cover design: Russell Punter
Research assistant: Georgina Andrews

CONTENTS

Who built the pyramids?

Tens of thousands of ordinary Egyptian men, led by architects, engineers and other experts. Most of the builders worked for the king for a few months every year as a sort of tax.

Step Pyramid

How old are the pyramids?

Incredibly old. They were built nearly 5000 years ago. There are over 30 left, and many are in amazingly good condition.

Desert police, called Medjay, patrol the western frontier with big dogs.

Where are they?

In Egypt, on the West Bank of the Nile, Egypt's great river.

A few people live in the desert oases - small green areas, with water and a few palm trees. They trade salt, cattle and crafts.

The Nile Delta. It's very green and marshy here.

Mediterranean Sea

Forts on Egypt's frontiers keep out invaders.

Great Pyramid and Sphinx

Stone for the pyramids is quarried here.

Red Sea

Memphis, the capital of Egypt in the Old Kingdom

Everybody travels by boat in Egypt. You can see a lot of Egyptian boats on pages 20-21.

Nearly everyone lives and farms in the Green Belt, all along the Nile.

Away from the Nile, everywhere else is desert. Egyptians call it the Red Land.

Trading ships set out from here for Punt in East Africa.

Thebes, the capital of Egypt in the New Kingdom

This is the Valley of the Kings. It's where the later kings were buried, after people stopped building pyramids. You can find out more on pages 8-9.

Just south of Egypt are Nubia and Kush. For a long time, they were ruled by Egypt.

The Nile is a very long river. It begins in the mountains and lakes of East Africa.

 2

Gold is mined here.

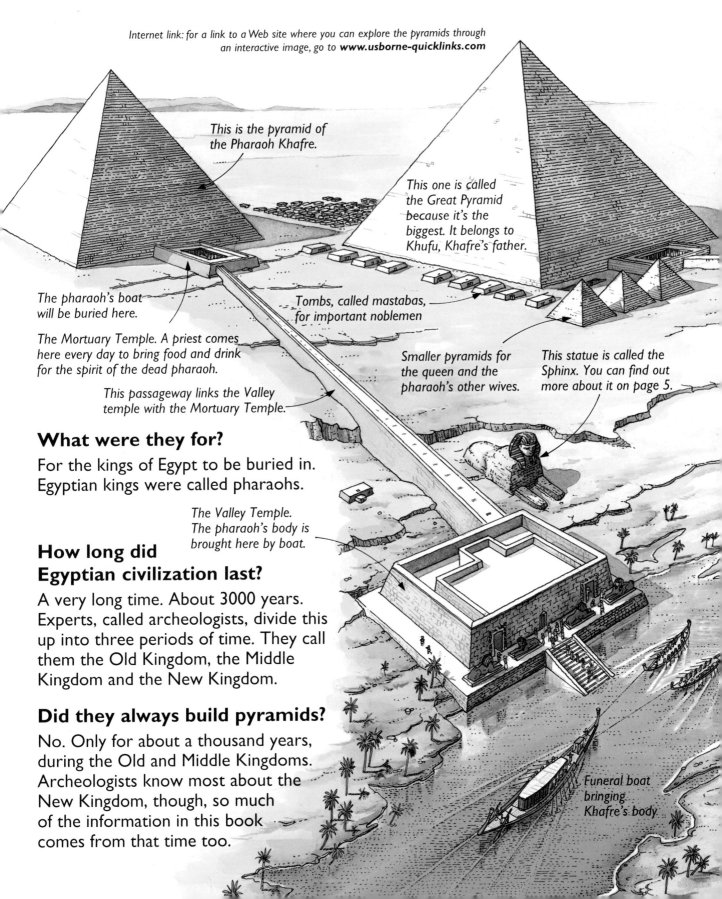

Internet link: for a link to a Web site where you can explore the pyramids through an interactive image, go to www.usborne-quicklinks.com

This is the pyramid of the Pharaoh Khafre.

This one is called the Great Pyramid because it's the biggest. It belongs to Khufu, Khafre's father.

The pharaoh's boat will be buried here.

Tombs, called mastabas, for important noblemen

The Mortuary Temple. A priest comes here every day to bring food and drink for the spirit of the dead pharaoh.

This passageway links the Valley temple with the Mortuary Temple.

Smaller pyramids for the queen and the pharaoh's other wives.

This statue is called the Sphinx. You can find out more about it on page 5.

What were they for?

For the kings of Egypt to be buried in. Egyptian kings were called pharaohs.

The Valley Temple. The pharaoh's body is brought here by boat.

How long did Egyptian civilization last?

A very long time. About 3000 years. Experts, called archeologists, divide this up into three periods of time. They call them the Old Kingdom, the Middle Kingdom and the New Kingdom.

Did they always build pyramids?

No. Only for about a thousand years, during the Old and Middle Kingdoms. Archeologists know most about the New Kingdom, though, so much of the information in this book comes from that time too.

Funeral boat bringing Khafre's body

Why are pyramids pyramid-shaped?

Good question. No one is absolutely sure. The very first pyramids had steps up the sides. Experts believe this was meant to be a giant staircase to help the dead pharaoh climb to heaven.

Later pyramids had smooth sides – perhaps to look like the rays of the sun. The Egyptian sun god Re was one of their most important gods.

The blocks of stone are dragged up the ramp.

Men pour water onto the ramp and put logs under the toboggans. All this helps them move more smoothly.

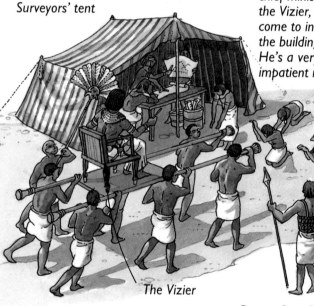

Surveyors' tent

The pharaoh's chief minister, the Vizier, has come to inspect the building work. He's a very impatient man.

The workers are hoping he'll be pleased with the progress.

Can you spot the irritating fly?

The Vizier

Carpenters

How big are they?

That depends. Some are not very big, but others are enormous. The Great Pyramid is as tall as some skyscrapers. At 146m (480ft) high, it's the largest stone building ever. It contains over two million blocks of stone.

Aren't they a little big for tombs?

The Egyptians didn't think so. They thought their pharaohs were so special that they had to have the biggest and best of everything. Also, the higher the pyramid, the closer they would be to heaven.

How were they built?

By dragging the huge blocks of stone up huge earth ramps. Experts disagree about exactly how these were arranged. But the ramps were probably raised and lengthened every time a new layer of stones was added.

Internet link: for a link to a Web site where you can see some of the different ways the building ramps might have been arranged, go to **www.usborne-quicklinks.com**

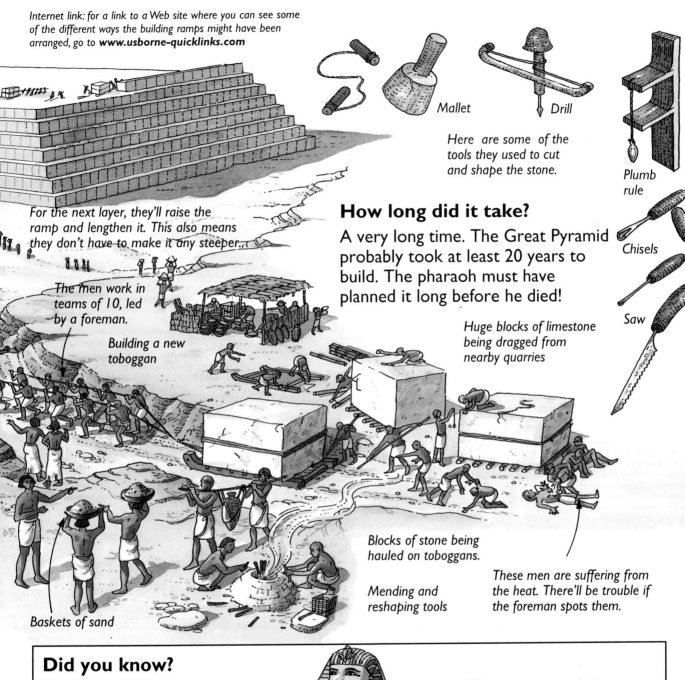

For the next layer, they'll raise the ramp and lengthen it. This also means they don't have to make it any steeper.

The men work in teams of 10, led by a foreman.

Building a new toboggan

Baskets of sand

Mallet

Drill

Here are some of the tools they used to cut and shape the stone.

Plumb rule

Chisels

Saw

How long did it take?

A very long time. The Great Pyramid probably took at least 20 years to build. The pharaoh must have planned it long before he died!

Huge blocks of limestone being dragged from nearby quarries

Blocks of stone being hauled on toboggans.

Mending and reshaping tools

These men are suffering from the heat. There'll be trouble if the foreman spots them.

Did you know?

Next to the Great Pyramid is an enormous statue of the pharaoh with a lion's body. It is called the Sphinx. For years, people thought the Sphinx contained hidden secrets.

They suspected there were chambers built inside, with ancient books of wisdom and magic. But we now know that the Sphinx is mostly solid rock.

What was inside a pyramid?

Not much (considering how big pyramids are). The insides are mostly solid stone, with long narrow passages. The pharaohs were buried with all kinds of amazing treasures, but they were all stolen long ago.

What is a mummy?

A body that is embalmed or preserved, so it doesn't decay, even over thousands of years. The Egyptians believed that doing this would mean that the person could carry on living in the Next World.

How did they preserve the bodies?

By finding ways of drying them out. Follow the pictures to see how they did this.

These pictures show how a mummy is made. In the background, you can see an outline of the Great Pyramid sliced in half.

1. First, they take out the internal organs, such as the heart and lungs, and put them in jars called canopic jars.

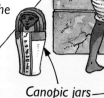

Canopic jars

Natron

2. Then, they cover the body all over with a salt called natron, to dry it out. After several days, the insides are stuffed with linen, sawdust, natron and sweet-smelling herbs and spices.

Burial chamber

3. Next, the body is wrapped tightly with bandages, with lucky charms called amulets between the layers. They use huge amounts of bandages.

Passageways

Anubis mask

4. Finally, a priest comes to say prayers. He wears a mask on his head to look like the jackal god Anubis, god of the dead.

6

Mummies in the New Kingdom were put in a nest of two or three human-shaped coffins, like these. These were put inside a huge stone coffin, called a sarcophagus.

Painted with pictures of gods and goddesses and picture writing (called hieroglyphics)

Outer coffin

Inner coffin

Mask fits over face

Bandaged body

The coffins buried in pyramids would have been simple box-shaped ones, like this one, with much less decoration.

Can you spot a pair of eyes on the coffin? They allow the mummy to look out by magic.

Why is it called a mummy?

The name comes from *mumiyah*, the Arabic word for bitumen, a sort of tar used on modern roads. When archeologists first found the bodies, they thought they must have been dipped in tar because they were so dark.

Didn't the mummies smell bad?

Not if the embalmers worked quickly before the body had a chance to decay. After it had been dried out and properly stuffed, it would have smelled lovely!

Were ordinary people mummified?

No. It was far too expensive for anyone except the royal family or top officials. But archeologists have found literally millions of animal mummies. These were animals who represented a particular god or goddess. They include cats, dogs, birds, baboons and crocodiles.

Mummified cat

7

Why did they stop building pyramids?

Nobody knows for sure. It might have been because pyramids were so enormous that they attracted all the robbers for miles around. They were also very expensive to build and needed a huge number of workers.

Were all the pyramids robbed?

They were completely cleaned out! Within a thousand years, every single mummy and piece of treasure had been stolen. Pyramid designers tried all kinds of tricks to stop the robbers, but they still managed to get in.

The Chief Priest rides on the funeral boat. He's burning incense. It smells nice and is supposed to carry prayers up to heaven in the smoke.

These women are priestesses. They cry at all the funerals.

Where did they bury their pharaohs after that?

In tombs cut deep inside rocky cliffs in a hidden-away valley called the Valley of the Kings. But, even though these tombs were difficult to get at and heavily guarded, in the end most of these were robbed too. Can you spot three robbers lying in wait?

This is a funeral procession to the Valley of the Kings.

This chest contains the canopic jars. You can find out what they are on page 6.

These soldiers are meant to be on guard, but they are having an argument instead.

Pharaoh's coffin

The Queen and her two children. The boy is the new pharaoh.

What were the tombs like inside?

The best ones were absolutely amazing. Rooms crammed with treasures made of gold and precious stones, clothes, furniture, pots, pans, statues, paintings, writings and even books. The walls and ceilings were brightly painted all over.

Pharaoh's chariot

This man is upset because he has dropped a valuable box.

Food, furniture, jewels and treasures for the tomb.

This snake is making the horses nervous.

How do we know so much about the Egyptians?

Because of all the things they left in their tombs. The hot, dry climate meant that everything dried out, instead of rotting away.

These are just some of the things the archeologists found inside the tomb of the young pharaoh Tutankhamun.

Is there really a mummy's curse?

No, of course not. It's just some silly gossip that spread just after Tutankhamun's tomb was discovered, over 70 years ago. Lord Carnarvon, one of the leaders of the expedition, was bitten by a mosquito, got blood poisoning, and died suddenly. A few people who liked a good story began to suggest that the pharaoh was angry at having his tomb disturbed and had put a curse on the archeologists.

Who ruled Egypt?

The kings, or pharaohs.
They were so important
the Egyptians even believed
they were gods. Each
pharaoh was supposed to
be descended from the sun
god, called Re, who was
the very first King of Egypt.

Were the pharaohs rich?

Enormously. Egypt was
a very rich country and
the pharaoh owned
absolutely everything
in it. He had not just
one, but several
palaces and he moved
from one to another.

Pharaoh

Queen

A scribe (you can find out what he does on page 30)

This courtier's fan is made of the very best ostrich feathers.

Gifts of copper, wine and oil for the pharaoh

Like everyone else who meets the pharaoh, these visitors from Syria are bowing very low.

Guards

These two men in long robes are called viziers. They are the pharaoh's most important advisors.

What did he wear?

Flowing robes and amazing jewels. He
had several different crowns. Most days,
he wore a gold headband with a vulture
and a snake made out of jewels. On
special occasions, he wore a double
crown. (This was two crowns in one.)

Vulture and snake crown

Double Crown

Red Crown of Lower Egypt (the north)

White Crown of Upper Egypt (the south)

Did he sit on his throne all day?

No, he was far too busy. He was in charge of the government, law, trade, and foreign policy. He was also the chief priest and army commander.

Here the pharaoh is inspecting sculptors building a new statue.

Paintings on the walls show scenes of life in Egypt.

One of these soldiers has just spotted a mouse.

Pillar decorated with hieroglyphs (Egyptian writing)

Visitors from Nubia (a land south of Egypt) with gifts of gold and ostrich eggs

This baboon doesn't want to meet the pharaoh.

Did the pharaohs have many wives?

Yes, but only one queen. She was usually the eldest daughter of the last king and queen.

Doesn't that mean he married his sister?

Yes, or his half-sister. This didn't seem odd to the Egyptians. They believed the queen was descended (like the king) from the sun god, Re. This meant she had to be a member of the same family.

Could a woman become pharaoh?

Not normally. If a very young boy became pharaoh, his mother could rule on his behalf. There was one queen, however, who actually called herself King of Egypt. Her name was Hatshepsut and she ruled successfully for many years.

Hatshepsut riding in her war chariot

Where did the Egyptians live?

In villages on the banks of the Nile. Very few Egyptians lived anywhere else.

Why not?

Because the rest of Egypt was just a huge, hot desert. The Nile gave people water to drink and wash in. Deep floods made the land fertile and good for farming.

Didn't peoples' houses get flooded too?

Not unless the house was too close to the river. Most were built on higher ground, away from the banks. But, if the flood was much bigger than usual, animals, people and villages could be swept away.

Village

This man is cooling down with a refreshing drink.

This house has been badly damaged in a flood.

This man is suffering from the heat.

Fishing boats

Flint-bladed tools called sickles

The children are collecting the grain the men have missed.

Lunch arriving

This pole with a bucket is called a shaduf. It raises water into the fields.

This flute player is entertaining the harvesters.

This dog has run off with some of the picnic.

How often did the Nile flood?

Every spring, when rain and melted snow flowed into the river from the mountains in Ethiopia, south of Egypt. It made it so full that it overflowed and flooded the land. After a few weeks, the water level sank, leaving behind rich, fertile soil.

What did they grow?

All sorts of things. Melons, pomegranates, grapes, dates, figs, beans, peas, onions, garlic, leeks, lettuces and cucumbers. The main crops were wheat and barley for making bread and beer. They also grew flax, for making linen for clothes.

Did the farmers have tractors?

No, but they had strong oxen for pulling blades to break up the soil, and donkeys for carrying grain.

Did they keep animals?

Yes, all kinds. Cows, sheep, goats, pigs, geese, ducks and pigeons.

The best fields are closest to the river.

Can you spot the monkey? In fact, he's not stealing the dates. He's been specially trained to pick them.

The farmers have dug ditches and canals between the fields, to store floodwater and water the crops.

Granary for storing grain

This man has had a little too much beer with his lunch.

A difficult donkey

The cows are being made to stamp on the grain to separate it from the husks. This is called threshing.

These people are winnowing – tossing the grain in the air to separate it from the husk (the hard outside bit).

What did they do after the harvest?

Get ready for the next one. For a start, the ditches that carried water to the fields had to be mended. Then, many farmers were sent off to work on one of the pharaoh's building projects – perhaps to build a pyramid.

What were their houses like?

That depended on how rich the owners were. All Egyptian houses were made of mud brick, with wooden roofs covered with plaster and palm branches. Most had just one or two rooms, but rich people had cool, spacious villas, brightly painted inside, with gardens and pools.

The servants live here.

The stable for the horses is at the back.

Grapevines

Wine press

Grain stores

Bedrooms

This enormous villa belongs to an extremely important man. You can find him in the reception hall receiving visitors.

Reception hall

The gatekeeper lives here. He keeps out unwelcome visitors.

These monkeys are helping the men to pick the dates. Of course they eat quite a few themselves.

This girl is taking an offering to the gods in the shrine. This is a sort of small private temple.

How did they keep the houses cool?

Any way they could. Most houses had very thick walls and only very small, high windows. This helped to keep the sun out. Some houses had air vents on the roof too.

What was their furniture like?

Scarce. Even rich people didn't have much. Most people sat on stools (chairs were very special), and used chests to store things.

Simple wooden table

Chair made of ebony (an expensive dark wood) decorated with gold and ivory

Painted wooden chest

Central hall. They're having a party here on page 19.

In the kitchen, they're busy making lunch.

Noisy geese

The roof is a good place to relax.

Brightly painted pillars

Cattle pens

Well for water

Pottery lamp

The pool is not for swimming in. It's meant for the fish.

Musicians playing

How did they light their houses?

With lamps, made of clay or stone, which burned linseed oil. These lamps only gave off a very dim light though. They would have needed an awful lot of lamps to light their houses as brightly as ours.

This lamp is made of marble and belongs to a pharaoh.

Did they have bathrooms?

Not like ours, but keeping clean was very important to the Egyptians. Most people washed regularly in the Nile. In an expensive villa like this one, there was a stone-lined room where a servant poured water all over you. This was the nearest people got to having a shower.

Can you guess what this is?

It's made of stone and it doesn't look very comfortable, but it's what the Egyptians used instead of a pillow. Apparently they slept very well on them.

Did they care about fashion?

Most people were too hot to bother – but rich people spent a lot of time and money on looking good. Unlike today, though, their fashions didn't change much for about a thousand years.

These are the sort of clothes people wore in the Old and Middle Kingdoms.

Fancy kilt

Linen dress with shoulder straps

Hair padded with ornaments for a special occasion.

A long kilt like this one means this man is old or quite important.

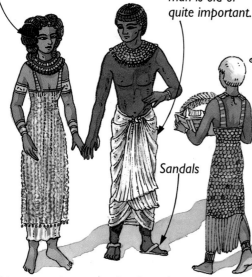

Sandals

This woman is wearing her best dress. It has hundreds of sparkling glass beads sewn onto it.

The barber has left a long braid of hair on this boy's head.

Men wore kilts like these, made from cloth wrapped around and tied at the waist.

How did the styles change?

The dresses and kilts became looser and more flowing. Hairstyles were longer too, with a lot of braids and curls.

Children and adults often shaved their heads to keep them cool.

These are the sort of clothes people wore in the New Kingdom.

Underneath his wig, this man is probably bald.

Flowing cloak

Flowing, pleated dress, gathered with a belt

Tunic over kilt

What were the clothes made of?

Linen, from a plant called flax. The flax was spun into thread, then woven into cloth on a loom. Most material was probably plain and undyed, though some people did wear patterned clothes.

Where did they wash them?

In the Nile, of course! They beat the clothes on stones to get rid of the dirt. There were no irons so they were probably left to dry flat in the sun.

These people are weaving on an early loom. Later ones were upright.

Internet link: for a link to a Web site where you can search Egypt for jewels in an interactive game, go to www.usborne-quicklinks.com

Did they wear jewels?

Yes, absolutely everyone did. Men and women, rich and poor. They were made of many different materials: gold, silver, pottery, faience (a sort of glazed pottery) and semi-precious stones, such as turquoise and lapis lazuli.

Beaded collar

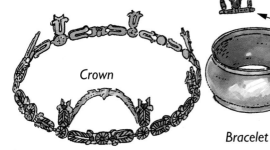

Rings

Crown

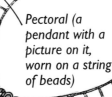

Bracelet

Pectoral (a pendant with a picture on it, worn on a string of beads)

Bracelet

Armlet

Did they wear perfume?

Yes, lots of it, made from flowers and scented wood soaked in oil. They also rubbed perfumed oil all over their bodies, to stop their skin from drying out.

Earrings

Mirror made from polished metal

Chest for keeping cosmetics in

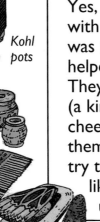

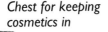

Kohl pots

Did they paint their faces?

Yes, both men and women outlined their eyes with dark green or grey paint called kohl. This was not just to look pretty – it helped keep away flies too! They also put red ochre (a kind of clay) on their cheeks and lips to make them redder. You could try to make yourself up like an Ancient Egyptian, using face paints.

Comb

17

What was Egyptian food like?

Very good. Their farms provided a wide variety of fruit and vegetables, meat, milk and cheese. People also caught fish in the river, and hunted wild animals and birds.

The people below are preparing food for the party on the page opposite.

What food did they like best?

Sweet things, probably, such as cakes, pastries and fruits, washed down with barley beer or fruit wine. They had at least a dozen different types of beer. The most expensive was imported from Syria.

Where did they do their cooking?

Outside. It was far too dangerous to cook indoors. They used sticks, dried grass and animal dung as fuel.

Monkey enjoying juicy pomegranates

This boy is about to get an eyeful of fruit juice.

A rat's nest

Fan to keep the fire burning

One of the goats is having salad for lunch.

This party is taking place in the villa you saw on pages 14-15. There are a lot of foreign guests.

This guest is feeling a bit left out. He doesn't speak much Egyptian.

Chargrilled fish

Spit-roasted goose

Lotus blossoms make the room smell nice.

Rolling out the dough

A goose with a temper

Mud brick oven

The loaves will drop off when they are ready.

18 *This dog loves fresh baked bread.*

How did they keep things cool?

They didn't. The weather was pretty hot all year round and there were no refrigerators. So they had to eat everything quickly before it went bad.

How do we know what they ate?

Because some of the food has been found in graves. It looks very dried up now, after 3000 years or more, but archeologists can still tell what it is. Wall paintings of parties also give us an idea of what the food looked like.

More food from the kitchens

This dog loves stuffed goose.

This boy is going to bed. He's too young to stay up for the party.

All the food is being eaten with the fingers.

Can you spot the harp player?

The host and hostess are sitting on the raised platform.

Dancers

Lyre player

Flute player

A guest from Nubia

A well-fed pet

Jugs of pomegranate wine

This guest has come from Syria with some interesting gossip.

These monkeys are trying to play with this pet goose. The goose looks a little annoyed.

What were their parties like?

Well, they *look* wonderful. Huge dishes of delicious food and wine, musicians, jugglers and dancers, and expensively dressed people in their best clothes and jewels.

Did you know?

Servants put cones of perfumed fat on the guests' heads. The fat melted and ran down their faces. It might sound disgusting, but it was probably very refreshing. How many cones can you spot in the main picture?

Internet link: for a link to a Web site where you can try out an ancient Egyptian recipe, go to www.usborne-quicklinks.com

How did the Egyptians get around?

By boat, of course! The Nile was like a great highway, stretching up and down the country, with all sorts of different traffic. In any case, there were no roads.

Why not?

It was pointless to try to build roads in Egypt. They would have been covered and washed away by the floods every year.

This barge is carrying a huge stone statue called an obelisk. It's going to be put outside a new temple further down the river. You can see it in position on page 27.

What kinds of boats did they have?

Fishing boats, funeral barges, luxurious boats for the royal family, cargo ships for transporting things such as stone blocks for the pyramids, and passenger ferries (which were usually overloaded). Can you spot the man who has fallen out?

The wind in Egypt usually blows from the north. This means the boats with their sails up are going south. For the boats going north, there is no wind to help them. They are the ones rowing.

Sea-going trading ship

The big boat on the right belongs to a rich nobleman.

These fishermen are dragging a net between their boats to catch the fish.

These boats are made of papyrus, a type of reed.

Did you know?

These are the Egyptian hieroglyphs for "south" (or "upstream") and "north" (or "downstream"). Can you guess what they show? (Answers on page 32.)

This means "south".

This means "north".

Internet link: for a link to a Web site where you can find out more about Egyptian boats, go to **www.usborne-quicklinks.com**

How far did they sail?

Traders sailed to ports in the Eastern Mediterranean and the Red Sea. Some even went as far as Punt, a land in East Africa. They went looking for valuable myrrh trees (used for making incense).

An Egyptian expedition to Punt

Myrrh tree

How did they travel on land?

Most Egyptians walked. The very rich were carried on special chairs. Merchants used donkeys for carrying things.

Didn't they have horses?

Not for the first 1500 years. Even then, they were too expensive for most people.

Funeral barge

Carrying chair

Donkeys

Cargo boat

What did the Egyptians do for fun?

All sorts of things. They had no televisions or theatres, but they enjoyed watching royal processions and religious festivals. A popular way to relax was to spend a day hunting, fishing and picnicking on the river. For Egyptians, this was a little like going to the beach.

A tug-of-war shown on an Egyptian wall painting

What kinds of sports did they play?

As well as hunting and fishing, they enjoyed wrestling, fencing and energetic games like tug-of-war.

There are two men on the right hunting hippos. This is so dangerous, it usually takes a team of hunters to harpoon just one of them and bring it ashore with ropes and nets. These two must be very brave, and a bit mad, to try it alone.

Did they have any indoor games?

They had several types of board games, such as the two shown here, but nobody knows how they were played. They also loved singing, dancing and telling stories.

Senet

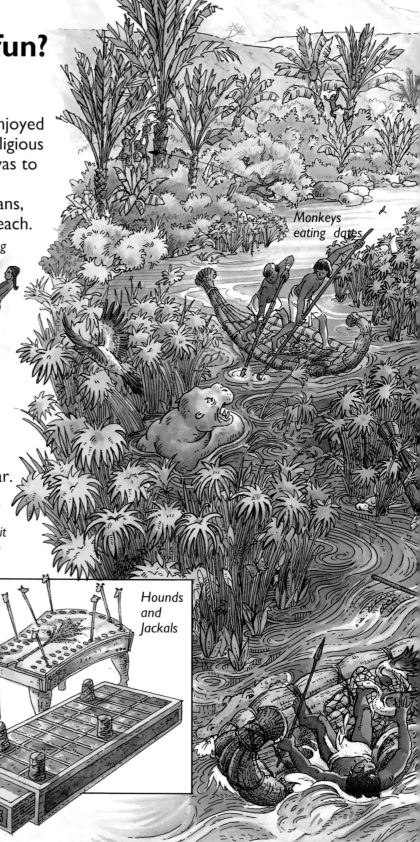

Monkeys eating dates

Hounds and Jackals

*Internet link: for a link to a Web site where you can play the board game Senet, go to **www.usborne-quicklinks.com***

Trying to tip over other boats is a popular sport.

A swim in the Nile is a good way of cooling off.

Papyrus reeds

Some people bring their pet cats hunting. The cats help to flush the birds out of the reeds.

The boats are made of papyrus reeds.

Luckily, this cat enjoys swimming.

What sort of toys did the children have?

Balls, spinning tops, dolls and wooden animals on wheels. Some toys even had moving parts – including a row of dancing dwarves and a dog whose mouth opened.

A handle opens the dog's mouth.

Hippo made of painted pottery

Leather balls

Did they play music?

Yes, but there were no radios or record players, so it was all "live". We know the words of some of their songs, but we have no idea what the tunes were like.

What types of instruments did they have?

Plenty of different ones. They had wind instruments, such as pipes and flutes, and stringed instruments, such as lutes, harps and lyres. There were also drums, cymbals, tambourines and castanets.

Lute

Castanets

Harp

23

Did the Egyptians believe in God?

Not one God, but dozens of gods and goddesses. The Egyptians were a very religious people. They carved and built thousands of statues and temples, and painted pictures of the gods all over them.

What were their gods like?

Very different from each other. Some were quiet and gentle, others were fierce and terrifying. Each one was linked with a special animal or bird. To make them easy to recognize, the Egyptians often painted them with the head of that animal or bird.

Amun, King of the gods in the New Kingdom.

Anubis, god of the Dead. He had a jackal's head.

Thoth, god of wisdom and writing, had the head of an ibis (a kind of bird).

Tawaret, a female hippopotamus, looked after pregnant women and babies.

Osiris, son of Geb and Nut, ruler of the Dead

Horus, god of the sky, son of Isis and Osiris.

Bast, a mother goddess. She is shown as a cat.

Geb, god of the Earth

Ma'at, goddess of truth and justice

Who were the most important ones?

Difficult to say. Isis, Osiris and Re (one version of the sun god) were among the most important ones. People believed Isis and Osiris had once been the King and Queen of Egypt.

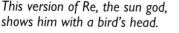

This version of Re, the sun god, shows him with a bird's head.

Isis, goddess of crafts, sister and wife of Osiris

Who was the most popular god?

Probably Bes the dwarf, because he was so funny. He made the other gods laugh and looked after people's homes

24 and children.

Were there any stories about them?

Yes, hundreds. Many gods and goddesses were related and married to each other. Their lives were full of feuds and fights and other adventures. You can read one of these stories on the next page . . .

Internet link: for a link to a Web site where you can find out more about Egyptian gods, go to www.usborne-quicklinks.com

There are many legends about Re,
the mighty sun god
and creator of the universe.
This one tells of how he nearly caused
the death of humankind,
and how he finally saved it.

The lioness and the red river

From the beginning, people had a great respect for Re. They feared him, for he was the most powerful god of all. Yet, as the years passed, there were those who thought Re must be growing old – and surely an old god must be weak and feeble?

Some people stopped their worship of Re altogether. Worse still, there were others who plotted his downfall. When this news reached the sun god, he flew into a violent rage. He ordered Hathor, the goddess of beauty, to go down to Earth immediately. Her mission was to destroy every single person who did not worship him.

Hathor went to Earth in the form of a lioness, with mighty paws, powerful jaws and terrifying teeth. She started by killing Re's enemies as instructed, but soon found she so loved the taste of human blood that she started hunting down and killing everyone. Even Re's most faithful followers were not safe from Hathor's thirst for blood.

When Re saw what was happening, he knew that he must act quickly to stop what he had started. While Hathor slept, he flooded Egypt with a very strong, red beer. When the goddess awoke, she saw the red beer and thought it was human blood. Full of excitement, she began to lap it up. Mixed with strong magic, the beer made Hathor very happy. Soon she was so happy that she forgot her mission, and her taste for human blood. She returned home with a headache.

On very rare occasions, the water in the Nile is a rusty red. Perhaps this is a reminder from Re that he may be old but is still all-powerful.
Or perhaps it is because the water carries red dust blown by the wind from the Sahara Desert.
Who knows?

Where did they worship their gods and goddesses?

Some family gods, like Bes and Tawaret, were worshipped at home. The more important ones had their own temples.

What went on in a temple?

Priests and priestesses conducted special services in front of a statue. (The Egyptians believed the god or goddess lived inside it.) Sometimes the pharaoh and queen were there, but nobody else.

This is the festival of Bast, the cat goddess. She is very popular with everyone.

Didn't ordinary people go inside?

No. They had to pray outside. People were only allowed in on very special occasions, such as after the birth of a child. They saw the statue on festival days, though. Then it was carried through the streets on a golden painted boat.

The statues in rows are called sphinxes. They have the bodies of lions and the heads of rams.

These tall, pointy things are called obelisks. They are monuments to the sun god.

The priests and priestesses are leading the way.

These cows are going to be sacrificed.

Flute-playing priestess

Statue of Bast

How many temples were there?

Probably thousands. Even today, you can see the ruins of hundreds of them all along the banks of the Nile.

Priests

Breakfast

Priestesses singing and dancing

What happened at a service?

First thing in the morning, the priests woke the god, washed the statue, covered it with perfume, dressed it and gave it food. There were prayers, music and dancing too. In the evening, the statue was put to bed.

The god lives in here.

*Internet link: for a link to a Web site where you can go on a virtual photo tour of Karnak temple, go to **www.usborne-quicklinks.com***

This is a New Kingdom temple. There are many outbuildings inside the temple walls – a library, a school, craft workshops and a house for the priests.

The walls are carved and painted all over with pictures and picture writing. You can find out more about the writing on pages 30-31.

This dog is terrified of cats – especially cat goddesses.

These boys are hoping for a closer look.

Did you know?

Some people used to put a carving like this, of a pair of ears, outside the temple walls. They hoped it would remind the god to listen to their prayers.

Did they believe in heaven?

Yes, but they called it the "Next World". All dead people were judged by the god Osiris. If they had led good lives, they lived happily ever after. For bad people, there was an evil, hungry monster waiting to gobble them up.

What were their towns and cities like?

Hot, dusty, noisy and crowded. They were very dirty too, as people threw all their garbage out into the street.

Didn't that make them very smelly places?

Surprisingly not. The heat was so strong that things dried up very quickly, and this stopped them from smelling too much.

Did they use money?

Not until a thousand years after pyramid times. Until then, people just exchanged things that were worth about the same. There could be problems though, if they disagreed about the price.

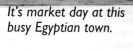

It's market day at this busy Egyptian town.

Fetching water

Did they have skyscrapers?

Not like modern ones. But building land was so valuable that many townhouses were very narrow and tall, sometimes as much as three or four floors high.

Unloading cargo

Where did people do their shopping?

At market stalls in the street. They sold everything from locally grown fruit and vegetables to pots and pans. There were refreshment stalls too, selling beer to thirsty shoppers. This was much thicker than modern beer (a little like soup) and very strong.

Was there much crime?

Egyptian towns and cities had their share of shady characters – robbers, murderers and people who tried to sell stolen goods.

Did they have prisons?

No. But criminals were often locked up in temples before a trial. (The walls were too high to escape easily.) Punishment included flogging, exile (being sent away) and death.

Can you spot the man ducking to avoid being splashed?

Temple

Cooking breakfast

This is the donkey that was causing trouble on page 13.

Did they have a police force?

Yes. It was called the Medjay. It was their job to keep law and order and catch criminals. In the country, they used big dogs to help them track down suspects. Can you spot the thief with the big fish?

Could the Egyptians read and write?

Yes. They were among the first to invent it, but very few people knew how. People called scribes had the job of reading and writing for everyone else.

An A to Z in hieroglyphs

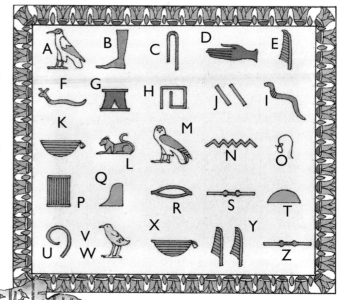

What did their writing look like?

Like pictures or signs. We call them hieroglyphs and there are over 700 of them. There are hieroglyphs for a single letter, some for a group of letters, and others for a whole word.

The Egyptians didn't have an alphabet like ours. But experts have invented one, just for fun, using the hieroglyphs that are closest to our letters.

Hieroglyphs can be written from left to right, or right to left, or in columns, as they are in this wall painting.

Always start reading from the direction the animal or people signs are facing. This means you read the alphabet above from left to right, as we do.

Egyptian painting follows special rules. People look as if they are painted from several angles at once.

The eyes look straight ahead.

The shoulders are drawn from the front.

People's faces, legs and chest are always shown from the side.

What did they write on?

Special paper, called papyrus (made from reeds) or bits of broken pottery. They used wooden brushes or pens to write with. They also wrote all over the walls of temples and other buildings.

Why did they do that?

Because they believed writing had special magic powers. Hieroglyph means "holy writing" in Greek. The Egyptian name for it was "words of the gods".

Pens

Papyrus

Inks

Internet link: for a link to a Web site where you can write your name in hieroglyphics, go to www.usborne-quicklinks.com

Did Egyptian children go to school?

A few boys did, but usually only the rich ones. Most boys worked in the fields, as soon as they were old enough, or learned a trade. Girls usually helped their mothers at home, but some of them had jobs too.

Boys at a temple school

They are using bits of broken pottery to write on. Papyrus is too expensive.

The teachers are scribes.

What different jobs were there?

Many Egyptians were farmers, but there were many different craftsmen and women too. A boy could also become a soldier. The best job was to be a scribe, a priest, a court official or a doctor. Egyptian doctors were so skilled that they were even famous in other countries.

Papermaker

Maid

Leatherworker

Carpenter

Mourner

Stone vase maker

Scribe

Musician

Weaver

Perfume maker

Dancer

Priestess

Doctor

Potter

Sculptor

Soldier

Write your name in hieroglyphs

You could write your own name, using the hieroglyphs on page 30. Pharaohs' names were written inside an oval shape, like this, called a cartouche. Egyptian words were spelled in a complicated way, so you won't recognize all the hieroglyphs. You should be able to figure out one of them though.

This is the cartouche of the pharaoh Meryre.

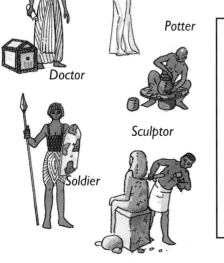

Index

Answers
Page 19
There are eight cones.
Page 20
One boat in sail and
one with its sail down.

First published in 1995 by Usborne Publishing Ltd,
83-85 Saffron Hill, London EC1N 8RT, England.
www.usborne.com Copyright © 2003, 1995
Usborne Publishing Ltd. The name Usborne and
the devices ♀ 🎈 are Trade Marks of Usborne
Publishing Ltd. All rights reserved. No part of this
publication may be reproduced, stored in a
retrieval system, or transmitted in any form or by
any means, electronic, mechanical, photocopying,
recording or otherwise, without the prior
permission of the publisher. Printed in Belgium.

Usborne Publishing is not responsible, and does
not accept liability for the availability or content
of any Web site other than its own, or for any
exposure to harmful, offensive, or inaccurate
material which may appear on the Web. Usborne
Publishing will have no liability for any damage or
loss caused by viruses that may be downloaded as
a result of browsing the sites it recommends.